ULTIMATE MACHINES

Helicopters

Rob Colson

WAYLAND

First published in 2012 by Wayland

Copyright © Wayland 2012

Wayland
338 Euston Road
London NW1 3BH

Wayland Australia
Level 17/207 Kent Street
Sydney NSW 2000

Senior editor: Julia Adams
Produced by Tall Tree Ltd
Editor, Tall Tree: Jon Richards
Designer: Ben Ruocco

British Library Cataloguing in Publication Data

Colson, Robert.
   Helicopters. -- (Ultimate machines)

   1. Helicopters--Juvenile literature.
   I. Series
   629.1'33352-dc23

ISBN-13: 9780750269087

Printed in China

Wayland is a division of Hachette
Children's Books, an Hachette UK company.

www.hachette.co.uk

Picture credits
1 Ikiwaner/GNU, 2 MD Helicopters, 4 US Navy,
5t PJF/Shutterstock, 5br US Coastguard, 6
Patrick Wang/Shutterstock, 7t Kevin Tracey/
Dreamstime.com, 7b Sean Moffitt/Shutterstock,
8l Ikiwaner/GNU, 8-9 NJR ZA/GNU, 9tr Monkey
Business Images/Dreamstime.com, 10 Digital
Vision, 11t US Air Force, 11b US Navy, 12 Wong
Chee Yen/Dreamstime.com, 13t Heike Brauer/
Dreamstime.com, 13b Steven Love/ Dreamstime.
com, 14 US Navy, 15t Corsair262/ Dreamstime.
com, 15b US Army, 16 Reuters/CORBIS, 17
Ken Babione/istockphoto, 18 MD Helicotpers,
19t MD Helicopters, 19b MD Helicopters, 20l
Meoita/ Dreamstime.com, 20-21 Paul Fearn/
Dreamstime.com, 21b John Mathys/Dreamstime.
com, 24 Corsair262/Dreamstime.com

Contents

→Vertical take-off

A helicopter is a flying machine that uses spinning blades called rotors to take off and fly. These spinning rotors allow helicopters to take off vertically, hover in the air and fly both backwards and forwards.

Helicopters can take off from ships or the tops of buildings. They can land on fields or even on the sea. They are widely used by the military, the police and emergency services.

An SH2F Sea Sprite helicopter comes in to land on a helipad at the rear of a warship. The Sea Sprite has sensors that allow it to search for submarines.

Amazing design

To take off and stay in the air, an aircraft needs to produce a force called lift. A helicopter produces lift using its rotor. The blades of the rotor spin at high speed. The blades are made in a special shape called an aerofoil. As an aerofoil passes through the air, it makes a downwards force that pushes against the air below it. The air pushes back against this force to produce lift, and the helicopter takes off.

The centre of the rotor is attached to the motor, which makes it turn. The rotor has between three and seven blades, which produce lift as they spin.

The first helicopters

The very first helicopter was made by French inventor Paul Cornu in 1907. It rose 2 metres into the air, but soon crashed. Thirty-five years later, the first mass-produced helicopter, the Sikorsky R-4, was made in the USA. The R-4 could reach heights of 3,700 metres, and had a top speed of 140 kilometres per hour.

The Sikorsky R-4 was developed for the US Navy during World War II. It was used to fly rescue missions and to carry out emergency evacuations.

Sea King

The Sea King is a medium-sized transport helicopter. It was designed for use by the navy, but it is also used by civilian services, such as the coastguard and mountain rescue services.

Sea Kings are used in search and rescue missions in the mountains and at sea. The underside of a Sea King is specially designed so that it can float on water like a boat.

Search and rescue

The Sea Kings that are used for search and rescue are fitted with thermal imaging equipment. This can spot people a long way away by detecting their body warmth. The crew includes paramedics who provide emergency medical treatment to people who may have been exposed to the cold for many hours.

An RAF Sea King demonstrates a rescue at an air show. A paramedic is lowered on a winch to pick up a person in the sea.

TECHNICAL DATA

Years of production
1969–1990
Engine **2 turboshaft engines**
Main rotor **5 blades**
Tail rotor **5 blades**
Crew **2 crew plus 27 passengers**
Empty Weight (kg) **6,207**
Maximum take-off weight (kg) **9,525**
Top speed (kph) **209**
Rate of climb (m/s) **10.3**

A Sea King patrols the coast of Cornwall in the UK. The Royal Air Force runs a 24-hour service that can respond to emergency signals from people in trouble at sea.

Amazing design

All helicopters suffer from a problem called torque. This is a force caused by the spinning of the main rotor, which pushes the body of the helicopter in the opposite direction. Most helicopters overcome the problem of torque with a tail rotor. The tail rotor produces a force that works against the pushing force caused by the main rotor. This stops the helicopter from spinning out of control.

The tail rotor of a Sea King is set on the left side of the helicopter's tail section.

AW109

The Agusta AW109 is a small, high-speed helicopter. It has a wide range of uses, including emergency services such as air ambulances.

In 2008, pilots Scott Kasprowicz and Steve Sheik flew right around the world in an AW109 in just 11 days, 7 hours – a world record. They flew at an average speed of more than 270 kilometres per hour.

Amazing design

Helicopters take off vertically when the blades of the rotor rotate horizontally. To fly forwards, the rotor has to be tilted forwards so that the force it produces pushes both downwards and backwards. When pilots want to accelerate very quickly, they can tilt the whole helicopter forwards, as shown above. Lightweight helicopters, such as the AW109, accelerate more quickly than heavier craft, making them ideal for use by emergency services.

Air ambulance

Helicopters are often used as air ambulances. They can quickly reach the scene of an accident, and can also reach patients in remote areas. Speed is very important to air ambulance services, which is why the AW109 is often used. It has space inside for two patients, three medics and medical equipment.

The AW109 is a Class 1 performance helicopter. This means that if one of its two engines fails, it is able to fly and land with just the one engine. This makes it a very safe helicopter to fly.

TECHNICAL DATA

YEARS OF PRODUCTION **1971–present**
ENGINE **2 turboshaft engines**
MAIN ROTOR **4 blades**
TAIL ROTOR **2 blades**
CREW **1 crew plus 7 passengers**
EMPTY WEIGHT (KG) **2,000**
MAXIMUM TAKE-OFF WEIGHT (KG) **3,000**
TOP SPEED (KPH) **285**
RATE OF CLIMB (M/S) **9.8**

9

CH-53

The CH-53 is a heavy-lift transport helicopter. It is used by the military to carry troops or cargo, such as weapons or vehicles, over long distances.

The helicopter was designed for use by the US Marine Corps, but is now used by many armies around the world. It can carry cargo on the inside or from a hook underneath the fuselage.

Amazing design

The Super Stallion is the largest version of the CH-53 helicopter and it is one of the largest helicopters ever built. The Super Stallion can fly 2,000 kilometres without refueling, but even then it does not have to land. It can take on more fuel from a ship sailing underneath it or an aeroplane flying alongside it.

A CH-53 refuels in mid-air. It takes on fuel through a hose at the front, which is attached to an HC-130 Hercules plane flying next to it.

Minesweeping

One of the most important jobs carried out by heavy-lift helicopters such as the CH-53 is to clear mines from the sea. The helicopter drags a mine-sweeping sled along the surface of the water. The sled detonates (explodes) any mines floating in the water to clear a safe path for ships to follow. The helicopter flies at a safe distance above the water so that it is not damaged by the explosions.

A CH-53 helicopter drags a mine-sweeping sled through the Persian Gulf to make the area safe for ships.

TECHNICAL DATA

CH-53 Super Stallion

YEARS OF PRODUCTION
1974–present
ENGINE **3 turboshaft engines**
MAIN ROTOR **7 blades**
TAIL ROTOR **4 blades**
CREW **5 crew plus up to 55 troops**
EMPTY WEIGHT (KG) **15,071**
MAXIMUM TAKE-OFF WEIGHT (KG) **33,300**
TOP SPEED (KPH) **315**
RATE OF CLIMB (M/SEC) **12.7**

EC130

The Eurocopter EC130 is a small, single-engine helicopter. It has large windows so that the pilot and passengers can see what is around them.

The EC130's design makes it very popular for sightseeing tours, because it is easy to spot sights that are below the helicopter. The rear seats are placed on a raised platform to give passengers the best view possible.

The EC130 is also used by police surveillance squads. Its large-window design allows the pilot to follow suspects as they move along the ground beneath them.

TECHNICAL DATA

YEARS OF PRODUCTION **1999–present**
ENGINE **1 turbine engine**
MAIN ROTOR **3 blades**
TAIL ROTOR **Fenestron**
CREW **1 crew plus 7 passengers**
EMPTY WEIGHT (KG) **1,378**
MAXIMUM TAKE-OFF WEIGHT (KG) **2,427**
TOP SPEED (KPH) **240**
RATE OF CLIMB (M/S) **9**

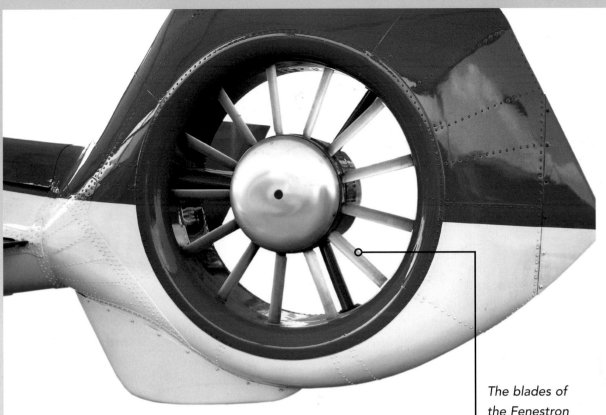

The blades of the Fenestron are spaced unevenly. This helps to reduce noise.

Amazing design

Instead of a normal tail rotor, the EC130 is fitted with a device called a Fenestron. A Fenestron is a fan inside a cylinder. It has up to 18 small blades, which spin round at high speed to produce the force that stops the helicopter from spinning (see page 7). The Fenestron makes a lot less noise than a normal tail rotor, and this makes the ride more enjoyable for the passengers.

Helicopter tourism

Helicopters can carry tourists into places they would not normally be able to reach. The Eurocopter EC130 is used to fly visitors around the Grand Canyon in the USA, allowing them close-up views of the canyon's spectacular rock formations. It is a very quiet helicopter, which makes it ideal for flying around national parks, where it does not disturb the wildlife.

Chinook

The Boeing CH-47 Chinook is a heavy-lift helicopter that has two main rotors. It is used by the military to carry troops, vehicles and supplies to the battlefield.

The body of the Chinook is more than 12 metres long, which is much longer than most helicopters. Its two rotors are positioned at either end of the body.

Amazing design

The Chinook's two rotors spin in opposite directions. Each rotor cancels out the torque caused by the other one, keeping the helicopter steady without the need for a tail rotor. This design is called a tandem rotor, and it keeps the long helicopter balanced and stable during precise manoeuvres.

TECHNICAL DATA

YEARS OF PRODUCTION **1962–present**
ENGINE **2 turboshaft engines**
MAIN ROTOR **2 rotors with 3 blades**
TAIL ROTOR **None**
CREW **2 crew plus 44 passengers**
EMPTY WEIGHT (KG) **10,615**
MAXIMUM TAKE-OFF WEIGHT (KG) **22,680**
TOP SPEED (KPH) **315**
RATE OF CLIMB (M/S) **7.7**

The Chinook can carry bulky cargo, such as jeeps, trucks and even small aircraft, suspended from ropes underneath it.

Dangerous moves

Chinooks are used to carry troops into dangerous and difficult places. If necessary, troops can climb out without the helicopter even landing. This is called a pinnacle manoeuvre. The back wheels are balanced on a rock, while the front of the craft stays in the air. The troops exit the helicopter at the rear.

Skycrane

The Sikorsky S-64 Skycrane is designed to pick cargo up and put it down again in the right place, just like a crane.

Skycranes can carry large structures to remote or hard-to-reach places. They may be used to lift electricity pylons high up into the mountains, or to carry concrete segments of bridges out to the middle of a river.

Amazing design

Skycranes are often used to help put out forest fires. A container full of water is attached to the underside of the helicopter. It then hovers above the fire and sprays the water over the flames. The helicopter can carry 10,000 litres of water at a time, the same amount as two large fire engines.

The Skycrane can use a long hose to suck up water from nearby lakes before dropping the water onto a forest fire.

YEARS OF PRODUCTION
1962–present
ENGINE **2 turboshaft engines**
MAIN ROTOR **6 blades**
TAIL ROTOR **4 blades**
CREW **2 (pilot and co-pilot)**
EMPTY WEIGHT (KG) **8,724**
MAXIMUM TAKE-OFF WEIGHT (KG) **19,050**
TOP SPEED (KPH) **203**
RATE OF CLIMB (M/S) **6.75**

A Skycrane can carry a load attached to its fuselage or from cables underneath. The fuselage is strengthened with thick metal so that it can carry the extra weight.

Long legs

The Skycrane looks very different from other helicopters. It does not have a body behind the pilot's cockpit and this makes it look like it has very long rear legs. This space behind the cockpit is used to fix water containers to fight fires (see opposite) or to hook on large pieces of cargo.

MD520N

The MD520N is a single-engine helicopter used for a wide range of missions, such as aerial surveys and police patrol.

This helicopter does not have a tail rotor. Instead, it is fitted with a system called NOTAR ('NO TAil Rotor'), which is much quieter than a tail rotor.

The MD520N is a popular choice with police forces around the world. Police officers can even ride on the helicopter's skids allowing them to leap off quickly when it lands.

Police helicopters

Police forces use helicopters for many different purposes, including traffic control and supporting officers on the ground. Police helicopters carry equipment such as infrared cameras, loudspeakers and digital street maps. The MD520N is a very quiet helicopter, so it causes a minimum of disturbance when patrolling over cities.

TECHNICAL DATA

YEARS OF PRODUCTION
1991–present
ENGINE **1 turboshaft engine**
MAIN ROTOR **5 blades**
TAIL ROTOR **None**
CREW **1 crew plus 4 passengers**
EMPTY WEIGHT (KG) **719**
MAXIMUM TAKE-OFF WEIGHT (KG) **1,519**
TOP SPEED (KPH) **282**
RATE OF CLIMB (M/S) **9.7**

Large pieces of glass all around the cockpit give the pilot a good view of what is happening on the ground.

Air is pushed out of a slit in the tail of the helicopter to produce a sideways force.

Amazing design

The NOTAR system uses a fan inside the helicopter's tail section. This fan pushes air out through a large slit on one side of the tail (as shown on the left). The air produces a sideways force to counter the pushing force created by the main rotor (see page 7).

Hybrid copters

Hybrid helicopters combine rotors with features that are normally found on an aeroplane. These include wings to provide lift or a propeller to provide thrust.

Gyrocopters are small craft that can be put together at home from a kit. They fly over short distances. Tiltrotors are large machines that can fly faster and farther than helicopters.

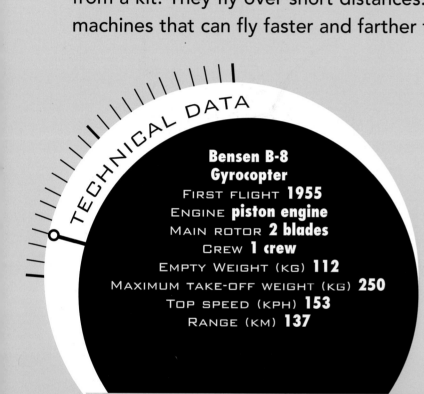

TECHNICAL DATA

Bensen B-8 Gyrocopter
FIRST FLIGHT **1955**
ENGINE **piston engine**
MAIN ROTOR **2 blades**
CREW **1 crew**
EMPTY WEIGHT (KG) **112**
MAXIMUM TAKE-OFF WEIGHT (KG) **250**
TOP SPEED (KPH) **153**
RANGE (KM) **137**

Spinning blades

A gyrocopter looks like a helicopter, but its rotor is not powered by the engine. Instead, a propeller at the back pushes the gyrocopter forwards, and this movement through the air starts the rotor spinning. This spinning gives the copter lift so that it takes off into the air.

V22 Osprey
YEARS OF PRODUCTION
2006–present
ENGINE **2 turboshaft engines**
ROTORS **2 rotors each with
3 blades**
CREW **2 crew plus 24 passengers**
EMPTY WEIGHT (KG) **15,032**
MAXIMUM TAKE-OFF WEIGHT (KG) **23,860**
TOP SPEED (KPH) **463**
RATE OF CLIMB (M/SEC) **16**

*As a tiltrotor comes in to land, its rotors are tilted
to point upwards. This allows it to land at small
airfields or on helipads.*

Plane and copter

A tiltrotor is a cross between a
helicopter and an aeroplane. The
aircraft has a pair of rotors on its
wings, which can be tilted to give
either upwards lift or forwards thrust.
Tiltrotor craft combine the speed of
an aeroplane with the versatility of a
helicopter. With a range of more than
1,000 kilometres, a tiltrotor can fly
twice as far as most helicopters.

Glossary

aerial survey
The collection of information about an area by taking photographs of it from the air, using helicopters, planes or balloons.

accelerate
To increase in speed.

efficient
Using energy without wasting effort. An efficient machine is able to produce a lot of power without using too much fuel.

evacuation
The rapid removal of people from an area, normally due to an emergency such as an earthquake or a flood.

fuselage
The main body of an aircraft such as a helicopter, which carries the crew, passengers and cargo.

heavy lift
A large, powerful helicopter that is able to carry a heavy cargo.

helipad
A landing area for helicopters, with a hard flat surface and well away from dangerous obstacles. A helipad may be placed on the ground, on a ship or even on the top of a building.

lift
A force that pushes aircraft up into the air.

mine
A weapon that explodes when an object knocks into it. Mines may be placed at sea to blow up enemy ships.

propeller
A fan that is found on aircraft and ships. As it spins, a propeller produces forwards force, or thrust, to power the craft.

rotor
The part of a helicopter that spins. The rotor produces lift as it spins. Most helicopters have two rotors – a main rotor and a tail rotor.

sled
A craft or vehicle that has a smooth underside so that it can slide along the ground or water.

thermal imaging
A system that uses heat sensors to create an image of the world according to how hot objects are. Thermal imaging can be used to find people in the dark.

thrust
A force that pushes an object forwards. A helicopter produces thrust by tilting its rotor forwards.

torque
A turning force that makes an object spin.

versatile
Easily adapted to many different kinds of tasks.

Models at a glance

Model	Years of Production	Number Built	Did You Know?
Sikorsky R-4	1942–1944	131	In 1944, the first helicopter rescue in wartime was performed by a US army R-4 in Burma.
Westland Sea King	1969–1990	344	After the 2004 tsunami in Asia, Sea Kings helped by carrying medical teams to remote villages.
Agusta AW109	1971–present	about 50 per year	The AW109 was originally developed as an air ambulance to operate in the mountains of Switzerland.
CH-53E Super Stallion	1974–present	115	The Super Stallion is nicknamed 'The Hurricane Maker' by sailors due to the wind its rotor produces.
Eurocopter EC130	1999–present	more than 100	Eurocopter asked tour operators what they would like from their helicopter when designing the EC130.
CH-47 Chinook	1962–present	more than 1,000	First used by the US Army in Vietnam in the early 1960s, the Chinook is still in active service 50 years later.
S-64 Skycrane	1962–present	97 made between 1962 and 1972	A Skycrane was used to lift the radio antenna to the top of the CN Tower in Toronto, Canada.

Websites

www.exploratorium.edu/science_explorer/
roto-copter.html

A step-by-step guide to making your own rotor-copter out of paper. See how it spins when you throw it, then read an explanation of the science behind what is happening.

helicoptermuseum.co.uk

The website of the Helicopter Museum in Weston-super-Mare, England. With photos and details of the more than 80 helicopters in the museum's collection, plus the kids' comic strip *Heli-Heroes*.

www.military-aircraft.org.uk/helicopters/

A site dedicated to military aircraft, with photos and information about military helicopters from around the world.

science.howstuffworks.com/transport/flight/modern/
helicopter1.htm

Illustrated explanations of how helicopters work, plus videos of helicopters in action.

Index

ULTIMATE MACHINES

Contents of all titles in the series:

WAYLAND